Congratulations, Rhododendrons

Congratulations, Rhododendrons

Mary Germaine

ANANSI

Published in Canada in 2021 and the USA in 2021 by House of Anansi Press Inc.
www.houseofanansi.com

House of Anansi Press is committed to protecting our natural environment. This book is made of material from well-managed FSC®-certified forests and other controlled sources.

House of Anansi Press is a Global Certified Accessible™ (GCA by Benetech) publisher. The ebook version of this book meets stringent accessibility standards and is available to students and readers with print disabilities.

25 24 23 22 21   1 2 3 4 5

Library and Archives Canada Cataloguing in Publication

Title: Congratulations, rhododendrons / Mary Germaine.
Names: Germaine, Mary, author.
Description: Poems.
Identifiers: Canadiana (print) 20200342851 | Canadiana (ebook) 20200342886 |
ISBN 9781487008680 (softcover) | ISBN 9781487008697 (EPUB) | ISBN 9781487009199 (Kindle)
Classification: LCC PS8613.E755 C66 2021 | DDC C811/.6—dc23

Book design: Alysia Shewchuk

House of Anansi Press respectfully acknowledges that the land on which we operate is the Traditional Territory of many Nations, including the Anishinabeg, the Wendat, and the Haudenosaunee. It is also the Treaty Lands of the Mississaugas of the Credit.

We acknowledge for their financial support of our publishing program the Canada Council for the Arts, the Ontario Arts Council, and the Government of Canada.

Printed and bound in Canada

For my parents and teachers

Contents

Part One

Ode   3

Some History of This   5

Marion's House   6

March of the Penguins   7

The Cliché Inventor   8

In the Lounge of the Overnight Ferry from Port Sydney
    to Port aux Basques, the Television Flashes   10

Lyrics to Wake Up Arcade Fire   13

Ekphrastic   14

I Didn't Love You   16

Valediction   18

Lourdes   20

The Reception   22

The Look on Your Face When You Learn They Make
    Antacids Out of Marble   23

For the Couple with Everything   24

"Let the Good Times Roll"   26

Good News   27

Crush Heaven   29

Scene Study   32

Augmented Reality Sandbox   33

Super Moon   36

Part Two

Upon Hearing How Long It Takes a Plastic Bag
    to Break Down   43

The New Routine   45

This Is the Day   46

Lines from Inside a Cage of Bees Which Are Not
    in Fact Bees Because All the Bees Are Dead Forever
    and Who Let That Happen Hey   47

Yeah, I Could Eat   49

Every Poem Where I Have to Pee in It Is a Pastoral   50

Coffee at Night   53

The Facts   55

End of July, Early August   58

Love Story with No Ark and Two of Nearly Everything   61

Since It's Better to Want What You'll Get in the End   62

The Gift, or "Things Will Be Fine"   63

Everyone in Paradise Is Coughing Their Heads Off   65

Take, for Example, This Hummingbird   67

The Rebel   68

Lies I'm Deciding to Live   69

Second Love   70

The Put-Pocket   72

Happily   73

Life Loves the Liver of It   75

Lines on *Substance and Shadow* by Charles Green Shaw   77

Notes and Acknowledgements   79

Congratulations, Rhododendrons

Part One

Ode

Congratulations, rhododendrons, on a job well done
this year. I'm in love
and your flagrant uptick in blooms has confirmed

a kind of religious order in me:
my inside and outside realms are identical.
They completely agree

in tense and tone, in depth, perimeter,
economy, and attention to moisture.
The humidity's gotten to everything

and everything I can imagine—useless questions
I would voice, wishes I would rather not,
worries—they're all laid out in plain sight.

From my place on the porch I can see
exactly which way that love will go.
There's a thousand different routes but they're all right

in front of me. Today has taken the shape
of a Möbius strip, soft as the porch breeze. As such,
there is only one boundary

and it divides what's real from what isn't.
Just between us, I don't think I'm the one
projecting, rhododendrons. I think you are

excelling at it. Which is fine with me.
It's not my job to calculate the difference between
my nerves and the white daytime moths,

or the gulp of sparrows tucked into the boxwood dark
and my own throat or lap or the heat of the flock
as it presses into the air. It's July. It's hot everywhere.

The tiger lilies jostle and nod. Who here
isn't doing their best to demonstrate a truly botanical
blind optimism? It's almost six o'clock.

Is it you or me, rhododendrons,
waiting with our red and pink faces
turned in all directions at once? Is it coincidence

I was walking through this neighbourhood last night
and my friend said rhododendrons were his favourite?
Occasionally, I had to notice, he smiles as thoroughly

as sunlight travels each vein of a leaf.
And then he smiled at me,
and offered to come by again tomorrow,

which is now today. You ruffle, rhododendrons,
and stick out all your necks. You wave as if
winter will never happen. You're right, it won't.

Winter is unthinkable now. A zillion flowers cover the sidewalk,
and there's way more still on the tree, to make sure something's always
looking up. And someone is crossing the street to me.

Some History of This

If properly wound, the robot friar will pace and kiss
his cross, and clatter out a *mea culpa*. Then again pace, then kiss—

Between an institution and a cliché, there's a narrow kitchenette
where a loose tooth and a hulking California strawberry try to reinvent the kiss.

As if to prove nothing changes, we talk nose-to-nose and every word
marks a new halfway point in the race to an infinitely distant kiss.

How do we forgive the guy who's out there on locust day, waiting to film
the last shaft of wheat that rainbow will bend to kiss?

Tonight's a drag, thinks the bartender, dumping ice melt from half-empty cups.
The sink's littered with lemon husks and more than one iridescently drowned kiss.

The price of barrels bobs and sinks. But a vending machine in Niagara Falls
will still make a souvenir tightrope with an American dollar and your honest kiss.

Lots of closets, and the view was stellar. We happily gave our first and last
and lived the best we could afford inside a rented kiss.

Coda in blue: a long line of Xs and Os I smeared under my name
so you won't forget what you're bound to miss.

Or not. The glass we jokingly pressed to our lips—it can only shatter once.
This is the handful of blood that the skin puckers to make a permanent kiss.

Marion's House

The clock above the stove is thirty-one minutes fast.
It's after breakfast now I'm not sure what I should
be doing. If the whole world feels on edge then
what is the precipice made of and what is the drop?

On the table three storebought blackberries
left in a dish the cat's all licked—it's almost too much. In fact
it is too much. This house is packed to the paint with nice stuff.
But it all seems in use I say to defend the porcelain elephant ring-holder

and towelling an elaborately painted chicken platter
trying to fit it oh anywhere don't worry Mary.
Kitchen's pretty well tidied. But say the whole world nosedives
it's not nothing it's the future we fall into. Is that helpful?

Well if everything wants to hang off its own lip
let it. Marion I don't think I'll ever understand your kitchen clock
but you're right in that we're ahead. In part because of your easy generosity.
And also I'd like to point out the little gold teacups that never leave

the top shelf. Buzz says we'll never use them and it's true. Too small
for proper tea and too gilt to work as one of those convex traffic mirrors
to warn: sharp turn. Marion how could anything be ever too much? The tea cups
pull on the tepid sun and use it to light the whole room.

March of the Penguins

The moral of the movie is that love does not just happen
every day. But in fact, it does.
Every job-stained day pinching to night, love
is the orange peels and chalky water cup you wake in,
panicking the soft checkered mountain
of unfolded T-shirts. Every desire you can think of
bounces headfirst off the kitchen light bulb,
which was left to burn up all night.
                                        I fell asleep. It's 5 a.m. and
love is happening and I still don't know how
to appropriately explain: I am jealous
of every minute you spend alone. I wish
I were that minute, small enough to rest on your sleep-weak mouth,
small enough to leave you, unnoticed, to examine
love from the frozen outside, and then to slip back in.

The Cliché Inventor

Was it like
falling in love?
Did she know
right away
she had something
forever
the second after
she leaned out
to say, Hey it is
raining cats and
dogs out there!
And her lover
or assistant or
gossipy stranger
met her at the window
saw the wildfire
spreading and thought,
I could do that
but with words.
And next went
the neighbourhood
up in smoke.

Someone must have
gone out to count
the hens and noticed
a glitter of
absolutely no worth.
His small felt tail
tucked between
his legs because
well where else

could he hide it?
That's how she
explained the scene
and then everybody
knew how
widely and reliably
true a remark
could be.

Or maybe it was
not like that
at all. Maybe
the cliché inventor
was in her workshop
with the curtains drawn.
She didn't see
the moon in June.
It was dark as
any other night
and not storming. No
bolt and thunder
of understanding
that she might
kiss and have
no one to tell.
And time won't
clear up anything
on its own
so she let
all the cats out
reasoning to herself
all grass
would be greener
under heavier weather.

In the Lounge of the Overnight Ferry from North Sydney to Port aux Basques, the Television Flashes

a new blue
unchorded and not sorry, an electrified powder

bursting from a plastics lab at Oregon State U.
The colour of a torched furnace. A breakthrough.

"But way more stable than other blues. Unfaded
by acid or heat. Brighter, reflective,

all around more useful. A paint this colour
could keep your house cool."

A mono-browed grad student explains how excited they are:
it will be easy to reproduce,

they'll have market share by June. Crayola's redesigned
the crayon box to make room. Effective immediately,

dandelion yellow is discontinued. And
they're hosting a contest: *Name That Blue!*

But how is anyone going to put a name to something they've never seen?
They won't even show it on the TV.

If you don't have a berth, you can spend tonight sitting up
in the lounge with the caged bar, and the Wi-Fi to peruse.

I've been gone six weeks, I'd like to know
what I'm coming home to. Or who.

It's not one of the establishment blues.
Not navy, not royal, not sky.

Not sapphire, turquoise, not baby,
not any other jewel. Not lapis lazuli.

It's the colour of I have no proof. Something wholly
unhinged from its instances: the parade boots,

Mother's ring, Matt McCarron's icy above-ground pool.
A work shirt I once really knew.

The colour for the question
of discovery versus invention. A blue for

is this only the beginning? Haven't we
been introduced? At a party. Isn't it

a wallflower colour
someone finally deigned to improve?

(Smashing the Coke goggles was all it took.) But
before that. How did Picasso make those women translucent

if he didn't have a palette knife full
of every possible hue?

His subjects are stripped so far down
they're missing even the glow of the nude.

Did the artist trying to sleep in his studio
sense something would always be missing?

Did knowing pay his ticket to ruin?
Did knowing send him home again?

It's the colour we never realized
we were missing it too.

Another ancient issue: if I am looking for something
I don't know, when will I see that I've found it?

The passenger deck is not a world I'm used to.
I settle for seasickness while the boat pitches

against the black
then darker black view.

I came up for something refreshing,
corrective, boldly pharmaceutical:

a patent-pending guarantee
for a brighter, better mood.

Don't rattle off the side effects
of a colour with no music,

no history, no present outside of a test tube.
Who's to say who's been true?

It's the last light I'm waiting to see
to believe it. Until I do, let's label this thing

"Maybe I'll call you later"
or "Maybe I'll call you soon."

Lyrics to Wake Up Arcade Fire

It's like a powerwash for your insides: Try Perma-Cheer.
There'll be no apricots in Kamloops this year.
And spoiler: no emotional intelligence
will get you what you're owed.
Unseasonably bare shoulders
are not it. But to take the edge off,
the farmers have crop insurance
in case of total crop failure which is
what we have here, he says.
If the trees are PTSDed, well
you can just imagine the people.
The apricot, the farmer goes on, is really
a canary in the coal mine. A reminder
the apricot's mealy lo-fi sound was
an early influence for Canadian indie-rock band the Arcade Fire.
I looked it up: it's not that "our hearts get tauter."
Sensing my concern, the banner proposes
Crazy Home Remedy For Unwanted Coal Belly:
Lift with your chin and watch this:
a leaf for all seasons floats downscreen.

Ekphrastic

Just a little bleeding, no reason to panic. Still,
better to get it checked out. Better to image because if
there's a problem, I'd never know it. My insides are dark to me
and likely a crawl space sculpture of empty gallon jars,
pool floaties, and a second prize set of
steak knives. Not enough to make a full-blown scare.
At the ultrasound clinic, I'm jokey against the taupe-lit
private room and the technician doesn't laugh. We're not
the fast friends some women become
in the minutes they have in common. So I don't say,
Hey, we use the same brand of condoms as you
are currently applying to that one-eyed instrument.
I lie back and shut my mouth.
She knows not every ultrasound checks for a baby.
This is only precautionary. No baby. Not as far as I know,
which I don't. What I thought was water wings
or a high-carbon double-forged full-tang Jamie Oliver knife set
could be anything. The technician says she's moving on
to my left ovary, and if I start to feel some discomfort, I should say.
Someone's cut two months from a calendar of bird paintings
and taped them to the ceiling for me.
The summer and winter landscapes are equally pillowy.
My bum lifts when commanded. The world could not be softer
for these cardinals, goldfinches, and black-capped chickadees.
They are padded into permanent frolic. An inch of snow
on the crimson birdhouse forms the most ethereal perch
for the cardinal gripping the eave, and a dangling mist
of berries collars the finches.
In summer, even-stroked lilies plush with yellow
lift the mixed flock to the apex of a moment
with no breeze. The greenery has too much give
for them to push off and out—they're stuck

in the camp of "let the work speak for itself."
Below the pictures there's a sign in the clinic font:
Technicians are not permitted to disclose their findings.
The birds face every direction except
each other's, the painter's, or the patient's.

I Didn't Love You

too much. Not beyond the light
curled around your hair, not past
the dry cough that knocks
at the edge of your every arrival.

I never loved your nonexistent fingernails,
the places you visit in dreams,
or even where you go now to get drunk,
though I used to think it was

cozy. Your mother's darkness, your clenching
future—these I ushered to join
your ricochet laugh in my ribcage,
your sleep digging into my arm. Whatever

you could not love of yourself
I took as I would with a tissue
sweep up the last few flecks
of glass from the floor.

Don't listen to our friends.
It wasn't too fast or too far.
I'm not heartbroken, and neither are you.

There was a glass harp strewn
across the table. A few people still
had a sip of the red left, and everyone
was trying to get the stemware

to sing, sliding their fingers along
the lipsticky rims. I didn't love you
too much then. I just loved
the way the room rearranged around

the crystal hum from your cup.
Holding it up to the lamp we could see
the sound was spotless, and clearly
it held us (at least a second) in return.

Valediction

If you don't love me then you'll be
just like everyone else
who doesn't. Who's not standing
beside me on purpose.
Who's touching me
or not touching with light
apologies as morning disperses—
the whole morning vibe beaten
to the thinness of a hair I find
knit in my shirt but at first
pretend not to notice and then pretend
not to know whose it is. Or was.
It's mine now and I'm leaving it
on the subway seat upholstery.

If you don't love me then there's no
seeing each other around,
not dressed like this. Look,
our separate fatigues
blend us with the scenery:
a scrim of any busy station,
a busy life in the blue distance.
The thinness of the late morning,
I find it everywhere now,
behind and before me.
I'm so deeply bored without you
and your way of leaning toward me
even as we moved through
different parts of the city.

But if you don't love me then I couldn't
care less when the train or bus
or whatever jerks under your feet.
The instinctive reach
that I would know you by
(if I were there) will find
the crush of a total stranger's
raincoat. This will happen
wherever you go.
A misplaced grin will widen
then drop. Don't bother
with trying—there is nothing
to explain to anyone.

Lourdes

Our lady of heavy
of steady water down rock
and dark pools of unknown
but often speculated depth

Our lady of lineups
of diabetic tube socks
backpacks colostomy bags
and snap-close leatherette

Our lady of neon
even the Catholic Church
gets shameless around tourists
Our lady of appreciating donations

Our lady of little soaps
in the hotel capital of France
it rains every day though
a bit of brass light shows
where her body's worn down

In the slow aisles of candles
umbrellas and water bottles
Our lady graces every label
It's a parlour attempt at omnipresence
but it still persuades

Our lady for the poor or stupid
queen of the one bended knee
braces of all kinds and stony smiles
Our lady of caves everywhere

We are here
like arrows like orphans
far from everything we know except
this world is not necessarily bound to another
and in the end neither are we

But believing is more or less
an attempt to fasten
We notice your own figure
is weighted with gold

A crowd waits in a downpour
to stand by what Sister Bernadette saw
Our lady please, please
every hotel and motel has a sign in six languages:
stay with us

The Reception

in the church basement
a shred of lettuce limps in the Miracle Whip
Wonder Bread sops the pickle juice
someone chewed the entire circumference
of her Styrofoam coffee cup
but left the coffee and the continents of creamer floating in it

to be fair the traffic's on everyone's mind
when the exhausted topics seep between the cousins
the tables down here are all uneven
and whispers roll down them like Shirley's blue eye

on the march back upstairs polished shoes pinch hot sympathy
to the parking lot to watch the hearse drive away
nobody knows whether or not we should wave
before rush hour swallows all our reasons to be angry

The Look on Your Face When You Learn
They Make Antacids Out of Marble

Who knows the name of the empire that took your arms, or the earthquake
that left you to drag your way, legless, to the top of the rubble.

Since then, your lucky friends became mosaics—the others
were ground to composites for IKEA kitchen countertops.

Of course, you too have had some work done: iron
posts replaced your iliac crest, oh, it was centuries

ago. And more recently, you were endowed prosthetic arms
reaching the whole length of the breathless hall gallery. Reclining,

you charge the light, and the light adheres. You wink
with every inch for the people milling past.

As I turn to go, you say, *Hey. Don't let
the grind get you down, babe.* And I think I hear

something else sputter and dissolve in your clean cut throat.
In the museum restaurant, a man finishes a spicy lunch.

From his pocket, he takes out a corner of your mouth, or maybe half your
formidable brow (who knows?) chews it up and leaves a bit of foil on the table.

For the Couple with Everything

Picturing the life you two are driving up and down the normal coast,
getting into the groove now of redwoods towering and marriage.

An artisan cutting board would go perfect with the new dinner routine,
so perfect it makes every salad a ceremony:

you're compelled to sing out *delicious* when the sliced tomatoes and cucumbers fan
a reminder you have so much to look forward to.

The cutting board itself is beautiful rectangles of walnut oak and cherry
resined together in the pattern of a modernist landscape

on the day of reckoning—I mean its odd stain-dark shapes
by some dramatic carpentry are finally unified and shot through with sunlight

which must have once slid past the foliage to sleep in this timber.
This wood has been cut to show off the white rings of age.

I would like to buy you two the evidence of decades of strength,
something dazzling that also functions as a cheese plate,

but what lousy taste to gift a metaphor that's always under a knife.
In no time the finish will be nicked away to nothing.

Last Saturday made it official: you two need each other and a need can get
such a jagged mouth on it—I think you're both so brave you deserve a trophy,

a gold lacquer vase soon to splash metallic light on your kitchen table.
It will pull at your cheeks with its gold mirror paint.

True a vase is where flowers go to brighten and die
like days if days had a shapely porcelain to crowd I'd bring you one.

But the only container that can hold the total embarrassment
of dawns and dusks as they slacken is the one who snores beside you so

Alex and Eduardo, please hold onto one another and be your own
bright guarantees. Since I am basically useless before your love

let me help with the decorating at least:
pick up flowers on the way home and let yourselves be surprised.

"Let the Good Times Roll"

Unlike the white stretch limousine
married to the crabgrass below a billboard
for motorboats and quads, the good times
could roll down Union, past Tim Hortons
and the Dairy Queen, the grandma and kid
yanking low helicopters off a tree. Let them.
As if it makes a difference. Good times
would if they wanted to
pick us up on the way to the beach,
past dark and I don't know, unravel
our underclothes into the river,
for once permitting the little splash
of liquor landing in a cup
that already has some liquor in it

Good News

Come see, go tell—
that's what it means to be a disciple.
But can you imagine

wading through the intersection, clipboard in both hands,
anaphylactic tongue Scotch-taped to your forehead,
all day on your feet

and lapping your blue pillow up all night?
Christ, you're a long way from the ocean,
from the loose rainbows

rising off cod bellies and the diesel shallows.
Once, your life was full as an egg. It had
an egg's little shine,

and it was simple believing there was something
brassy being polished inside. So when
the first instruction—

the one ahead of any discipline—
when the rule came down from without:
Be opened

who wouldn't fall apart? Who wouldn't
feel themselves getting carried away
by a march of fire ants?

Christ, there's just too many. Who
could make them each understand?
The good news

was never about the crowds, what they wanted and what they ate.
It wasn't the recovered wallet or the medical marvels. Not even
the little brother

who left us. His eyes, which were my eyes, turned red
as two dead dogs. That far gone.
When he came back—

miraculous, yes. All the bottles broke open at once.
Fortunately, a disciple is one who isn't afraid
to drink, then stand,

smiling at the relief in bloom across these faces, smiling
to reassure them when you start. When you have
the backyard's attention

you say what you always do: *Have you heard?*
All this—their faces shine and muddle like bruises—*this*
will be over soon.

To be a disciple means you can't prove what you know.
But you keep your eyes open and you promise you will
never fall asleep again.

Crush Heaven

When a loyal desire has suffered long enough,
and you decide to put it down, and you do,
the spirit of the crush is finally relieved
and floats off to hang out in crush heaven.

It's a mall downtown with a movie theatre in it,
so the building stays unlocked late.
The timeless faux-marble hallways
are exhaustively lit a dental white.

I should know—I went. Or was sent, I guess.
Chosen from the group for the impossible task
of getting to the liquor store in time.
I was thanked in advance with a hero's reward:

a phone number and the song of "See you later"
in my heart. This is how
a great love begins, I sparkled to myself
and swung glass door after door open.

("Nothing is difficult when you love"
my fortune cracked at dinner.)
The mall was bumping. Power-glossed
floors and columns bounced off each other,

and the crushes were everywhere:
unseasonably gorgeous, or plain but
probably terribly thoughtful. Possibly sober.
They had winning smiles, or well-cut clothing,

or else the virtue of a moment they just
happened to be standing alone.
In fact, they had all arrived alone, but the crushes
were mingling now, cool as hell,

they dissected the movies and themselves. *Interesting but
too slow. Overacted. Great scenery. The mother was fantastic.*
The crushes went on and on, hefting their dealbreakers
like you might switch the arm under a snippy terrier.

I'm sure it gets annoying toting around
one's fatal flaw. Every night in crush heaven
is spent talking politics, showing off
half-mashed popcorn in their molars. I saw someone

snoring in the food court, fluttering her lashes.
Some twisted a ring on their finger, two or three
rocked a stroller. Nobody was crying but
every single one of them clutched their side.

So none seemed to notice me. I slipped through
their afterworld unseen — even after
I saw a guy identical to Rick from Grade 10 English
and sung out *Hello!* half-accidentally.

What am I, invisible? But no,
my winter look was in each long mall mirror,
though maybe I was camouflaged by the escalator.
I also hum while I'm working.

It took forever to get out of that basement.
You know how malls become a maze,
and crushes have a terrible sense of direction.
I walked by the same dimmed storefronts

for who knows how long before
the Bloor Street exit appeared. I held the door
for the person behind, but when I looked back
I assured my future, and not a soul was there.

Scene Study

The bees in Harvard Square
make honey out of garbage:
pizza crust honey
Pepsi honey
Aquafina honey
shrieking child
sweat honey
Harvard Square is a hot and busy place.

God knows where these bees hive.
Maybe they sleep inside the newsstand
or up behind the security cameras.
Or maybe they go higher,
and hang off the giant clock
on top the bank. I don't know.
Maybe at night they hide under
empty scratch tickets
or the guy asking for change
and handing out cigarettes for free.

If there's a parable here, it's lost on me.
Sometimes a glob of mustard
is just resting on a man's golf shirt
and a commuter manoeuvres
drinking around a Starbucks stir stick.
Everything sucks
as much as it can.

Augmented Reality Sandbox

Genderless hands rifle
through the augmented reality sandbox
a live topographic map of mountains peaked with
is that imitation rust? No
real saturation sliding to a peachy-orange
looser rings of dandelion daffodil yellow
greens of diverse readiness
ribbon to ultramarine
the augmented reality ocean
unfurls in hand-dug channels
but doesn't splash out
over the particle board rim
even when our guide's arms extend
to gather half a mountain
drawing it close to a glowing
white golf shirt
raking in every grain
like they won
only to push it away again
as if trying to scrub the landscape clean
seems like a sandy waste of time
except then a sunset does
dissolve into the dry slush
a summit collapses and
no one is injured
the map buffers

while the soft demonstration hands
patiently reportion a range
installing well-known lines from the old countryside
fields and floods rocks hills and plains are made
to repeat themselves until they bleed

together to form sensational fjords
which also trail off
when a dizzying slope suddenly
plateaus in the centre
of the map the cursor still
doesn't blink for a second I think
I see a place I'd been to before
on a holiday with Sarah to an island
so tiny when we landed I was afraid for it
and worried our airplane would bounce off
skidding back into blue
for a week of rum
swaying and pineapple juice
we raced the sun down
to the water hoping to catch
the famous green flash
as it shot across the equator
if you find yourself that far south
you can sometimes see the sun
send one flick of new
light green as a Martian
along the last second of
the day's clear horizon
but we just
missed it every night

I count at least
nine green flashes in a minute
of the new map which turns out
to be like nothing I've seen on vacation
the augmented reality sandbox is bigger
than all of creation it has to be
to contain each illuminated speck
of earth plus the specks below
them plus our ever-touring attention

and yet the map fits nicely
inside the dimmed map room
where there's just enough
space for one person to shimmy
around its perimeter before
the video cuts off the hands
brush dust on their shadow khakis
a crucial gesture
the hands turn out to be
the only index for the map's scale
the only way we can
size up the depth
or relief we might feel

Super Moon

whatever moon
I think you're super
even if
you are waning
a bit not breaking
any records not like
you were Saturday night
everybody stepped out
with you hovering on
the tip of their tongues
knowing the last time
the earth and moon
were so close
a war was over
it was 1948
the number one hit
was "You Call
Everybody Darling"
by Al Trace and His Orchestra
people danced and you
moon tried to cut in
to get with some bright
swing of colour but
you weren't a sore loser you
got too caught in the groove
jived so resolute
the needle jumped
the acetate cracked
then nothing
and nobody
could be played again

everyone smoked in those days
and agreed it was quite a scene

you know what's super?
6:45 in the morning and I
have already missed one bus
and I'm racing around the corner
to try and catch another
hopefully and you
moon have the window seat
on a train moving
the opposite direction wait
no you're not
you're still in the backyard
a few blocks over behind
the house after house after
house flying past me
you are so brightly
eye-level I thought
you were a pop-up
billboard for cold medicine
or drive-thru banking
or a gigantic baseball diamond floodlight
for a crack of dawn pick-up league
but no you are
the real moon
chilling on a neighbour's fence
having overflowed their birdbath
your eight hundred
and seventy-third
bath today
you seem super
nearby but
we both must realize

I'm not fast enough
to really catch you
the morning always chaperones
our little meetings
I can hear her
purple slippers on the stair now god-
damn I am late for work

and forcing
big cold breaths
under my parka
at the bus stop
a couple with travel mugs
noodle into their own
morning routine
when you moon
lean right into the middle
of Massachusetts Avenue
for one minute
I only have eyes for you
all the other street lights
mean nothing
next to you my dumb
job my pissy mood
busted zipper on my friggin' coat
it all shrivels
while the seconds balloon
it does get boring
so when the bus rumbles
my eyes drop to it
and when the bus
pulls up I
give you one last
longish look

longer than my earlier
more struck look
my view stretched no doubt
by the calisthenics of the fact
we just can't
change each other
so I punch another
screeching fluorescent ride
and you dear moon
calling everybody darling
you ancient pervert you knew
by the light of your own scars
I couldn't stay
even if I wanted to

Part Two

Upon Hearing How Long It Takes a Plastic Bag to Break Down

Other centuries built cathedrals!
With arches, domes, and turrets
that spire into low heaven.
They drew faces out of eons of stone
and then gave every face eyes
brimming with non-questions:
Should they stay? Or should they go?
(Go where? Go how? It was the picture
of vanity.) Other centuries hung bells
strung with smaller bells as close as they could
get to an overlooking God so that
God might hear the racket
of the ground, the shakes of bronze
hitting bronze, or iron on iron,
whiplashing the wind some days hourly.
It brought the people together,
like the crumbs of a tablecloth, lifted
by its corners and carried off.

Those prayers have been answered. By now,
on earth and far over our heads
plastic bags smile and flag.
We built them to make it easy
to carry groceries, gym shoes,
shorelines, treetops, and dog shit.
And they do. And they will, until the end
of time, or the next five hundred years—
whichever comes first. I will be buried
and I'm not sorry some plastic will outstay
my appreciation of sunsets. I suspect even sunsets
will be garbage by then. Garbage: the definition
of unloved and unfuckable. So unlike us,

no matter how tight, how tangled we get.
Who hasn't licked that last bit of icing
off the Saran Wrap before tossing it
straight into a seagull's stomach?
Oh it's easy to panic over every
silent killer we should have thought of.
My own breakdown took about forty-five minutes.

But in the shadow of Notre-Dame-de-Grâce,
families are enjoying ice creams.
They're not worrying though they must
have heard about how everything convenient
will soon brittle to polyethylene dust
and ruin their children, who have already
zoned way out, gawking up
at the painstaking statuary of sinners.
The marble sins will be released
eventually into marble dust
which will become the ordinary dust
caking on tourists' sandals and tongues
and then going home with them
to their tiny fresh perspectives.
But plastic bags refuse to convert
to anything but permanent rubble.
Some days, it's tempting to rummage through
for what's been lost. And some days,
I too feel like getting away from it all
(away where? away how?) but when I try
I always get caught up, watching
a plastic bag waltzing to the seaside,
though there's no music to be heard.

The New Routine

I go to bed beside myself
and wake the same
The moon is silent on the shelf
I go to bed beside myself
He said the point was something else
He would not say my name
I go to bed beside myself
and wake the same

This Is the Day

and the very best thing about how the Lord
has made it: soon to be forgotten.
This day is softening
a callous on the brain—if there is a memory,
it is smooth grey slid beside the rest
in a stainless steel refrigerator warehouse:
one more in a row of Whirlpools.

I don't know—was there something about today
so enormous, luminous, not to mention absorbing
it could blot out the day before
at the same time as tomorrow? No.
In this "insane season of world history"
(as one recent birthday greeting put it)
each moment is another in the great chain-link

fence we dare not lick again.
If I had the whole day in front of me,
would I recognize it? Would I know
the hours by their light deflections?
There's always someone I'm forgetting
I should blame. Or maybe
thank. At some point, I saw
a stream of melted winter latticed by the sun.
There are no other details I can salvage
from oblivion. I'm sorry. Not one.

Lines from Inside a Cage of Bees Which Are Not in Fact Bees Because All the Bees Are Dead Forever and Who Let That Happen Hey

This is the night the Lord has made,
the wind and sour snow,
blades of fluorescence and jalapeno taquitos,
from 7-Eleven—all this
is the Lord's domain. These are the lines
the Lord has drawn to cleave
taquitos into the hot spin of being
instead of nothing. These
are the sidewalk cracks, these are the facts:
in the video, the crushed cornerstone
was the soft side of somebody's neck.
This is the flinch we live in,
half a breath long but looping
with the bass in the *Cops* theme song.

Anyone at 7-Eleven at 2 a.m.
is looking for a way out, or else
a way in. Cruising the aisles for some
crinkle-wrapped reason to say
Thank Heaven. Something marvellous
in our eyes. Bright and wide
open. Cheezies and chips,
energy drinks, phone plugs,
earbuds, eggs, and Big Gulps
the Lord has made. There are
rows and towers of itemized glare
and what else? Your patience
with us, Lord, is villainous

and tough as Plexiglas. The cashier bows
his skinny head and passes me
a waxed taquito. *Good night*
he says, not letting on whether
he sees a bright side I just can't
or he merely hopes he might.
Good night, he says again, setting me
in the broad place of his smile.
This is the gate. I ought to buy
a lottery ticket for his winning
cleft lip grin. I nod too.
Thank you. He buzzes to unlock
the unbroken glass doors and outside
the night also endures.

Yeah, I Could Eat

Who put the ogle in Google
Obviously World Vision doesn't care when I let flies crawl all over me
By its sheen I guess bluebottle
No I'm not itchy are you itchy
But we try and keep the screen closed while we're out here
Do pixels exist in the wild like the light on the water on the lawnchair you
    just sat in were those pixels
How come some lights are totally blockable and some lights are fire
A hangnail invades the panorama every time it's like wow what a beautif—
    wait what's with my cuticle
Apparently there's a space sickness astronauts get once they're back and it's
    because they've had some nirvanic appreciation of the ultimate blue
    marble then they land and just get saturated with traffic signals and
    cigarette butts on the beach
You know when you zoom in too fast
Face it a good reason is hard to search
For fifteenth time today YouTube tells me "Time has no meaning thanks to
    McDonald's New All-Day Breakfast"
Fine not every flashing sign has to mean something
But actually I just started seeing someone

Every Poem Where I Have to Pee in It Is a Pastoral

These roses smell like Chinese food.
Like, spicy. Greasy and
warm. It's unseasonably warm
for November tonight.

I've gotten myself so lost along a Boston
city limit, and I thought
that maybe stopping to smell these roses
might help to calm me down.

But what the hell kind of a place
grows a garden with MSG?
I can't find one single sympathetic reason
(nearby Chinese restaurant maybe)

for such a savoury smell. Not at this hour.
None of these windows are fogged
with fryer slick steam or chatter
circling around the bill.

Tonight is empty of even the clinging
soupy wheeze from the late regular
(heaven help him)
the waitress always blows off.

The glass that fronts this street, like the last,
and the street before that, is dark
except for the odd glare from the unmarked
cars speeding to the freeway.

No neon eddy invites me over
and over to somewhere glowing
O-P-E-N
Restrooms for Customers Only.

This is why everyone hates nature:
nothing to buy out here.
Plenty to smell but nothing good to eat.
Nobody knows that better

than the night-browsers, riding the crooked
wheel of their shopping carts
up and down the laneways, perusing for
who knows, finding wire hangers.

I guess I'm going the wrong way again
five or twelve blocks too late.
The more I walk, the more this night
coolly edges away

and some animal, night-like but rustier,
sidles into its place.
Too late now to take the T. Too far.
Boston's gotten bigger

by the minute, while I've been squinting I hope
to limit the distance between me
and the universal beacon
for late-night salvation.

But even 7-Eleven
is locking up. The girl
turns her back to count the till.
The Slurpee maker's dim.

Through my reflection, I can see
tomorrow's bananas
stacked into a pyramid,
and all the stems point down.

Coffee at Night

The tremor in the mug
holds its own electric shine.
This is how you get
to make light of the time:
drinking coffee
across the night shift
down at the minute factory,
where you assemble chances
in any shape you choose—
there are no rules
to stop you from cramming
extra bubbles in the bottle
or pulling each
metallic thread to a frazzle.
As long as you keep
half-busy. What's
keeping you up anyway?
What's with all the coffee?

The night collects
a tax for lingering
so long on your work:
overkneading one,
grinding another
too fine. A minute
can be fashioned
from anything
inside the triangle
of your lamplight.
The price
of a coffee at night
is the sound

first of your jaw
drilling deep
through the bones
of the middle ear.
Hammer, anvil, stirrup.
Then breaking
the calcium white noise,
a man's voice
boxes your building,
circles the block.
He screams, *Fuck YOU
I'M HUNGRY I'm
HUNGRY fuck*
plus some other words
you can't decipher
but you know
you'll have to pay for
later.

The daylight demands
a dither tax too.
When you finally see
tomorrow's shrivelling
afternoon, you'll have to
meet the sidewalk body
clenched to a question,
and it isn't *why*
or *when*. The body
isn't answered
by the loose hours
you hid in your pocket
bright as new copper.

The Facts

The first fact is I'm in love with my best friend's new wife,

there is no right place for my eyes to rest.

What I'm looking for is where a woman's lipstick goes

after it's left her lips and teeth,

carried by the light hiss of an *Excuse me* or *Please*:

a question mostly caught by the quick turn

in her hair. But where does the truth of her there—

first on the platform, then boarding a certain eastbound train,

then alighting where she needs to, at Christie, my home station

—where does the minute truth go when it loses its hold of her hand?

All clues are defectors,

and so are colours. Any colour may move on or withdraw

but never substantially disappear. For example:

the pixels the sun takes from lilacs lately

it returns to the suppertime sky,

as anyone this side of the street could observe from their staircase window, before returning themselves to chatter and the hot stove,

to CBC and CNN. It is not a great distance to examine—

in fact, sight is an excruciating medium

made all the more painful by the angle of my best friend's

new wife's reach across the table for the pepper mill.

The fact of her gesture, like everything else, is small and hard,

and getting away from us.

What I'm looking for is the place

where the facts reveal themselves in peace,

a place we can meet for relief.

Do not say it is only in memory that the happy truth persists,

when we can all see something better than memory is muscling through

this very conversation. Sorry, something's caught in my throat.

You'll have to excuse me.

While I was upstairs I couldn't help but notice

a dramatic and familiar shade of coral

was settling on the roofs across the way.

Maybe it's only the dust from the sun's end-of-day shrug.

But if that colour could get me closer to understanding

the swirl inside your near-finished cup,

or the kissed-up air that hovered briefly in the hall,

I have to follow. I have questions for everything

your mouth has ever pressed and left.

End of July, Early August

I. End of July

The river today is a drawer of diamond
drill bits the baby dumped on the floor.
Some things seem like they should be
fun but they're not. Build-your-own
birdhouse. Or the sun coming out.
The sun is not even pretending
it doesn't know that tickling is in
the encyclopedia of torture. The sun knows
without reading about it. The sun has been there.
Someone's laughing in panic because
he can't find his sixteenth of an inch of the river
and nothing else will fit. He gets
down on his hands and knees to look—
maybe it rolled off the deck. Or an ant
dragged it away like a dead friend.
Wild raspberries catch him instead.
He's the first to see them chubbied up
from the rain, fat pouches of hot jam.
They are leftover sex organs, after all.
The second raspberry has a honey coil
of hair in its centre. Another has a
downy feather. *Silly thimble fruit,*
a feather is not a finger, tut-tuts
the tickling expert, and snatches it.
The last raspberry has a little yellow
molar inside. Too small
to be a river tooth, and it's not
one of his, and it's not mine.
He can't use it. Unless—could this be

a sign? No. Or yes. As Jane says,
A sign may be but the sympathy of nature for man.
Sympathy for which man? I ask but Jane
doesn't answer. She's a stand of dark
forest herself. In love with a blinded man,
she's the definition of somewhere else,
only real under certain conditions. I wish I knew
where that river got to.
Andy hates when things don't work
as they should. I don't care very much
whether the raspberry bush feels for us or not.
I just want something to tear through
this mind-numbing humidity, something to make room
for a tiny brown breeze with red and pink on its edges
to circle the yard looking for nothing,
and find it and leave.

    II. Early August

There's one fat wish trapped in a rose bush
in front of an empty home reno.
The flower the colour of curdling cream
could be the last of the season
but the real question of a morning this chalky
is whether the wish arrived on its own
or if it was led by one white whisker
and set with the rose for safekeeping.

The answer's retrieved with a swoop to the sidewalk:
a foreign coin with foreign lettering
and the foliage of its nation. A serifed number 2
argues both head and crown have been
brazed together forever in a thumbnail
of copper and zinc. On the flip side,

a serrated bird of prey repeats my birth year, 1992,
before hotly continuing: *Every creature*
is a vessel for the creator's desire.

While I agree no one has ever
stamped money because they're satisfied,
and no one goes face and eyes
into the rose bush because they're not alone,
in August, the sun is a coin I find
impossible to spend, and I keep it on me at all times.
What can I say? I'm a sentimental.
Even in August. Even when I'd rather be
a PVC tube, abandoning my original purpose
to make the low hum of admiration
when the August huff passes over and through.

Love Story with No Ark and Two of Nearly Everything

Two plates, two forks, two glasses of white,
two questions and two answers,
(*Are you still holding your breath? Did you hear that?*
Must be the windchimes. Yes.)
a little dish, handmade in France, for the salt
in two pieces on the floor.
The salt is uncountable
and it's everywhere.
Two soft apricots
saved for dessert.

Since It's Way Better to Want What You'll Get in the End

Thank goodness my soul longs for justice,
and not Kit Kat bars made by child slaves.
I'm not dying for a Dairy Milk or Coffee Crisp—
my soul wants only the shadeless day
when the adults of the world line up to trade in
their shoddiest desires for a cool even keel,
giving up aerosol whipped cream and a workplace spanking
to stand alone for five minutes in an open field,
hoover-eyed but breathing through their noses for once.
Justice isn't blind. It's watching and it will know
perfect timing, just like a landmine does, jumping at its chance
to nibble the baby's perfect little toes.
Horrific. But aren't you glad? Ours are not the worst hungers.
Some souls long for forgiveness. And might forever.

The Gift, or "Things Will Be Fine"

A white elephant if there ever was one—
I see a crow in the Loblaws parking lot
and I just know, simple as a stoplight

it's a sign a sorrow's about to tear in here, and
pronto. *So you're a cynic?* I knew
you would say that. Now am I invited in, or what?

I'm not cynical, I'm starving. I'll take what's given.
If two crows are sharing the telephone post,
then a reasonable joy will land any minute,

and if three arrive on scene together, it means
a girl is waiting. These are just the facts,
true as the size and weight of a toothache.

I don't know. Listen, the first thing you learn
in the gifted program is whatever you count on
will add up to something. But eventually

I quit any augury involving feathers. Too formulaic,
and anyway, things were always heading south.
So now what? Besides house calls?

I do dreams, mostly. People are willing to pay all day
for someone to listen while they gather purple wool.
When women call me complaining

vacuum cleaners are chasing them down each night,
what they really need to hear is
stop sucking up so much shit at home.

And a nightmare about spitting teeth says
nothing except you're sick of being a cog
in your own life's soft machine. It's so obvious to me

if you dream of drowning more than once a week
then it's time to quit drinking. No one ever wants
to hear that but I have to call it like I see it.

I have a talent that makes men go blind, and the women
who have it are unbelievable
                    —*wait, what are you talking about?*

Last time I saw Cassie she was a mouthful of pills, and
who could blame her? But also, who would trust all her nasty
emphatics? Not everything gets to be the end of the world.

For example, the word FINE appeared six or seven times
on my walk over here. Will Katie ever come back?
Can't tell you that. But I know how things are going to be.

Everyone in Paradise Is Coughing Their Heads Off

That's what the television said about us!
Didn't mention it rained so hard the palm trees
lay down flush with the street! I didn't sleep!
And Christmas came anyway! With a message for every machine:
RISK OF FLASH FLOODING CAUTION THIS
IS A RECORDING. A pineapple! Wearing a Santa hat
and a bottle of Benylin outside our door! PEACE ON EARTH
the bells in the back of my head were ringing!
And it sounds like a miracle but! The TV says
the scenery's always decked red green gold and
sweeping the wooden single-lane bridge to town
out to sea! So the hotel staff are spending
the morning at home with their children
and we're all getting mai tais for breakfast for free!
They're self-serve! Fresh! Squeezed
from the relative humidity! Our Jacuzzis run over
and down to the beach! Where the kids are too busy
with their game of Survivor to remember their own names!
They've found curious furry seed pods and palm fronds
long as a man! What are their names, again?
Sweet angels draped with infinity towels
kicking up the dark sea to announce the end
of paradise! As if! We didn't know!
We knew! Vacation is over the minute
you get there! There's just one rule: take a picture
when the hibiscus finally opens
in our throats! Take a picture of the waterfalls like distant
pillars of smoke! And the jungle one wet beetle shell
shaking off some iridescence! Angels! Come here!

It's so precious we can all be together!
One more picture! For our friends back home! They'll never
believe that we felt so harmless! Hacking our lungs
and wicking our lounge chairs in the downpour!
Well you never know! The sun might come out
for our angels' blue faces! Another perfect day!

Take, for Example, This Hummingbird

I cannot keep holding forever
between the sure thumb
and forefinger of my mind
the fuchsia I caught cleaving
this morning's bright box.
You were turning from the balcony to say,
When is jealousy permissible
and when is it a sin to be jealous?
Nothing rests on my answer, I know
—least of all your marriage,
which is not exactly up
for discussion, nor all of a sudden
blessed by the entrance of a hummingbird,
though it is unequivocally a blessing
to hold its sequin breathing near.

The hummingbird moves so quick
in the trees it blends with the air
turning the whole morning a pastel
pink. What is a hummingbird doing
in the wet switches of December?
Again I'm aware there's no heft
in my answer. The hummingbird's
doing the same as it always is:
arching deep into something sweet
and very, very small.

The Rebel

slides ten dollars for the free pizza
on the table just as he's leaving.

A rebel will take anything as an exit
and while he brushes past you, steals your favourite

colour, saying it's always been his favourite too.
Cool. See you later. He has several porcelain gestures he uses

as camouflage even amongst his clumsiest friends,
those who know he also wears a permanent crown

slung across the wide of his back like a sunhat
which tipped off his head when he downed his glass.

The crown is made of rebelling back hair.
Tonight his eyes match the dinner plates, moving from hand to hand or

clattering to the floor. Some moves don't land as they're meant.
He breathes out some names like an apology sent

just after you've been relieved of the brass-edged rule
he just pulled open as a door and stepped through.

Here comes (or goes) the rebel—everybody loves him.
And the rebel loves with his eyes half-closed, half-open.

Lies I'm Deciding to Live

The beautiful are never broken-hearted very long.
Beyoncé is right: nothing real can be threatened. No one notices
when someone's only ten minutes late. One more won't hurt
and one fewer doesn't matter—except every plastic straw
finds its way eventually inside a sea turtle.
My mother was joking that time she called me a slut.
She didn't know you can't just make a joke like that.
I didn't know any better. Getting what you want too
soon isn't great either. Just a drop of club soda
gets out any kind of stain. No point in laying blame.
No need for anyone to get defensive. After all,
it makes sense.

Second Love

The only one to say my name like he knew
what it meant has long left. He knew it only
ever meant itself, a definition simple as north:
invisible and untradeable. You can always

take north in your most available hand and even if you don't
bring it back with you, people will think your gesturing is true.
I did. I let his small and pointed air
be the right answer, the only possible counterweight to steady

my double-bent gale-walk up the Prescott wind home.
My name was a thread. In those days,
I could be lifted on a thread. When he left, there was nothing to do
but twist inside my skin and twist in

borrowed beds. I drank tall glasses of amber holidays
with no end. Still, I found my way back, with my name
hanging wide open in front. It became shorthand for the blur
of fence posts and the harbour they pushed beyond.

My walks have no ocean in them now. But a small-mouthed
man seems glad to go along with me.
He's not a man of his word, or not of some. My name,
for example, means nothing

coming from him. It falls straight down the breathless gap
he offers his arms across. He calls me using the easy
cup of his hands. His whole comportment is an open hand—
I suppose you could say the same

for any number of men, so ready to grasp and turn,
and yet—this man's call I answer, starting
with the shock-white gossamer beneath my skin
that's ruffling to him. I'm letting myself become

a woman led by ruffles, as if ruffles were the only choice.
I'm not wrong. What else is there to trust
in a man without the measure of words? There's no true or false,
no north to hold against him. No harbour, no railing,

no reason anywhere for thinking it would be fair to say he just
doesn't get it, or that I'll never get gotten again.
There's only the two of us on this street. But that's not why
a second love doesn't need to speak

to lift me on his index finger so I can ride
shotgun in his shirt pocket for free.

The Put-Pocket

Weighing little more than a humid breeze,
and with hands as swift as two hummingbirds
making love, a put-pocket has hustled me

and pinned on my person small things at first:
a perfect one-inch slingshot twig, a raspberry rhinestone.
Then one day I found a king-size Kit Kat bar in my purse

and there's no other explanation—
someone bumbled by me on purpose to drop
that candy bar, and later, an uncapped pen,

a mood ring, a map of the Golden Horseshoe, a prop
poniard, twenty-eight dollars in loonies, a dime
bag of glitter, a house key, a combination lock,

and a loose-fitting wristwatch. They get slyer every time.
Last week, a kind word fit inside my egg salad on white.
Yesterday, an extra quarter note in my heart's resting rhythm.

Amateur suckers ask *Why me?* then forget.
When I catch that unswindling punk, I won't wonder.
There's only one way to level this debt.

I'll ink the put-pocket's fingers with butter,
fasten a bell to their thumbs,
zip-tie each wrist with the full moon's glare,

then I'll throw the dark windows of my house wide open
so the honest work can begin.

Happily

The happy couple overslept. They missed
the pre-dawn traffic crumpling
back into pumpkins, a signal for the end
everyone had been told to expect.

The bridge steel began coiling into salt water,
and the iron to blood. Most windows
had been made of sugar pane: the glass shook
when it dissolved to dark rum.

The foliage floated down to gold and the gold
softened to oily cotton—
even people's dental fillings unfurled,
breakfast tasted like shoe polish.

But soon that too softened to a sponge of relief
on their cankers and ulcers and cavities.
Those who had ached for feet got them
delivered as purple orchids

and daisies, so they Charlestoned on *congratulations*
and phone bill confetti. Songbirds exploded
into fireworks then flocked back into their bodies in time
for the chorus. The crackies quit barking.

And finally good men stepped out from the waiting
rooms and laneways where they had lived as
Lysoled furniture and dumpsters until they learned
their lesson. They did. And quietly

began to tidy the glitter while they listened:
someone was unswallowing a stone.

When they heard the throat singing they began their weeping
one thousand molasses tears.

When the tears hit the concrete, it inflated into bread
and butter, as something better
than gold, and way better than beanstalks, shimmied
up toward ever-after. It shone

like a well-rubbed abstraction, like a dream house
or a moral. This was the finale they all knew
was coming, just as they knew saw-toothed mothers
would one day be thwarted by yeast infections

and good mums would win full custody.
Gummy rodents opened wide
to huzzah the happy couple who waved
and were married with the sunset by lunch.

And then anyone checking the weather swooned
into dreamless sleep, still wearing their shoes.
They felt safe. Their faces untangled
like the newly cleaned coast.

When they woke, there would be a lot to do.
The future is terribly long.
But today, their faces are the only clearing
the next palace might be built upon.

Life Loves the Liver of It

Life loves the liver of it,
she says. Life loves the spleen,
tickles or heimlichs the esophagus
according to its need. Life loves a
shivering kidney with a split-second hot stun.

Life loves the lungs, their broad and leafy hurry,
their wet night rattle and the one hollow note
from behind a false wall, sounding
to let you know there's a secret passageway
beside you in the soggy bed.

Life loves the heart as you love
traffic and weather every ten minutes on the tens.
And its affection for the stomach is obvious—see
how life waves madly whenever you board the bus.
The obedient stomach waves back.

But the favourite's always been the liver. Life loves it
without ego, without trapezing its fabulous
five hundred vital functions. (We know, we know.)
Who said life was fair? Not the nerves—all of them—strung
along the swift and dip of a too-bright day.

Don't you love a hardback chair
after working twelve hours on your feet?
Use a plate if you're making a sandwich,
please. Come to the table. Listen,
bring the bottle we were gifted earlier.

It supplies its own tonic, don't worry.
And don't you start ragging on me.

I feel just fine. Life will always look
after me and my liver and I'll tell you
why: it has to. Life needs

to rest sometimes in the liver's fine-grained
seat: jealousy, wrath, and greed.
The heart can't take it, the stomach drops
to its knees. Luckily, nothing is stronger
than a sucker, and the liver is always ready.

If life tears at you and smarts, if say, a lunch guest
has talons and vicious news, and your lungs wither
and crumble apart—don't worry.
The liver may wince at the bitterness but
tomorrow it'll grow back for more.

Lines on *Substance and Shadow* by Charles Green Shaw

They seem to be essentially the same now,
flat against the gallery wall:
two torquing figures equally substantial,
equally shadowy in their readiness to fall
at the forest fire–tinged sun. The trees are gone
from here, or they're towering in uniform grey,
grey as the houses, their windows and starlings,
the school and main street. You can't tell
anything apart once it's crammed in this room
and a fire just ripped through town. What's left?
A jaundiced sun and two familiar concepts,
soft as we hoped that categories would be,
and waving us in with abstract sweater sleeves.

It's not clear which form would be better
to join: the taller one, substance,
seems rarer, or maybe just a whiter
slant of grey, turning to face the sun
or swivelling away as if searching for anyone
except its partner, shadow. Shadow,
the colour of something badly burned,
reclines or maybe always drapes itself
in a stingray's silhouette. If that grey
is the shoreline, holding off the grey sea,
then now's our chance to get away.
Follow me—I'm going with the dark
when it steals out of frame.

Notes and Acknowledgements

"Lines from Inside a Cage of Bees Which Are Not in Fact Bees Because All the Bees Are Dead Forever and Who Let That Happen Hey" and "This Is the Day" both heavily borrow from Psalm 118.

"This Is the Day" is a poem of gratitude for Angela Ferrante.

"The Put-Pocket" was Jordan Leech's idea way back when.

"End of July, Early August" quotes Charlotte Brontë's *Jane Eyre*, and "Life Loves the Liver of It" is quoting Maya Angelou.

Earlier versions of some of these poems appeared in *Riddle Fence*, the *ArtSci Effect*, and *The Walrus*. My thanks to the magazines' editors for the warm welcome.

I am so grateful to everyone at Anansi who helped me move the poems off my clipboard and into the world. Your efforts have been such a thrill for me. Thank you especially to Kevin Connolly for the insights, patience, and enthusiasm for the minutiae.

Most of this book went through a workshop at one time or another, and I am much obliged to everyone who read these poems carefully and graciously attacked them with a scalpel and once or twice, magically, with a corkscrew: Carmine Starnino, Robert McGill, Justin Andrews, Cody Caetano, Mitchell Gunn, Zak Jones, Helen Marukh, Sebastian Wen, the early readers at UMass, Eliza Ives, Grace Rebecca Taylor, Christine Wu, and Triny Finlay. I can't tell you how much these poems have benefitted from your intelligence and generosity.

One thousand thanks to those who have extended gentleness, jokes, suppers, unofficial writing retreats, occasions, suggestions, and wonderful, offhand remarks I wrote down without asking: Marion Cheeks, Sarah and Andy Lilly, Victoria Smith, Wyatt Hirschfeld Shibley, Andrea McGuire, Prescott, Tommy Duggan, Alex Grant, Alex Sarra-Davis, Mandy Pipher, Jess Elkaim, Lucas Boers, Nadia Khan, Sheila Mulrooney. The whole reason I wrote the poems was to make you people laugh.

I've had more teachers than I could possibly name here—so many people nudged me toward the right way, and many more laid the ground that made my writing possible. I am deeply grateful for their help.

Barb and Robin, thanks for all the "material." Thanks for letting me run with it.

MARY GERMAINE is a Ph.D. student at the University of New Brunswick.